READINGS:

JOHN AT PATMOS
and
A BOOK OF HOURS

CATHERINE de VINCK

READINGS

JOHN AT PATMOS

AND

A BOOK OF HOURS

ALLELUIA PRESS

By the same author:

— A TIME TO GATHER, Alleluia Press, 1967 and 1974
— IKON, Alleluia Press, 1972 and 1974
— A LITURGY, Cross-Currents, 1973 and 1977
— A PASSION PLAY, Alleluia Press, 1975
— A BOOK OF UNCOMMON PRAYERS,
  Alleluia Press, 1977 and 1978

© 1978, CATHERINE DE VINCK

ISBN 0-911726-32-2 cloth—ISBN 0-911726-33-0 paperback

Library of Congress Catalog Card No. 78-55341
Designed and published by ALLELUIA PRESS
  Box 103, Allendale, N.J. 07401
  and Combermere, Ont., Canada, KOJ ILO

PRINTED AND BOUND IN THE UNITED STATES OF AMERICA.

CATHERINE de VINCK

JOHN AT PATMOS

TO MY SON JOSE

*"All things were made by the Word. In the beginning, there
was neither mind nor matter. In the beginning was the Word.
St. John was properly the first Christian theologian because
he was overwhelmed by the spokenness of all meaningful happening."*

(ROSENSTOCK-HUESSY, *The Christian Future*)

INDEX OF FIRST LINES

JOHN AT PATMOS

AND to Patmos I came
   a place, ten miles by five
   of imagined isle on which to hear
   what shall be spoken.
Omens do not fall sizzling
on my plate: I must dig them up
like roots, scrape them clean
cook them in the proper pot.

The mind boils and bubbles.
Up from the sea, the sun hits
the skull, like an enormous rock.

I must be open
   the ring of my soul broken
   the seal of my being broken
   the body raked fine, a beach
   on which no one will stand.
Then a Word will be spoken
   —Patmos is the place, the spirit-space
   the meeting ground: here is where I begin.

✓   ✓   ✓

I was not listening
   could not be listening all the time:
the ear tires of the gull's cry
   of the wind rubbing against the trees.
I was not waiting: how long can you sit
   cross-legged under a Greek sun?
But I heard, closer than heartbeat
   a voice saying, "Child!"

1

Childhood is a distant station
lost in the mist of another land
but I could say yes, I am a child
alone on this isle, hearing full well
on Patmos the imaginary, the real call
louder than the waves, closer than heartbeat:
and here is where I begin.

                    ✓   ✓   ✓

I live in the wilderness. Around me
volutes of the shell, mouth of the cave
curve of the sea: soft shapes
I enter deep. I inhabit the house
of the conch, pass through
coral doors, wed the sea.

The voice cries, "Child, child!"
and I am at ease, I love what I find
the salt and the sweet of what I see:
the coupling of man and woman
     she of the wide thighs
     she of the birthing spasm
     she of the suckling babe.
The voice finds me, repeats, "Child!"
and I know I am the child born of Eve
     I am heir to a vanished garden.
I look on and on. The blood in my veins
telegraphs messages, taps codes
I decipher and understand. I see the face
of my first father, dark against foreign hills:
old Adam eating raw flesh
with great squared teeth.
The ancient mother combs her hair
with twigs, sits drowsily
by the grinding tools.
She is tired, cold: fire, uninvented
lies dormant in the heart of stones.

I weep over her: my tears freeze
fall in crystal drops. The ice-age girds
the world with silver chains, drives away
the paradise beasts. The herd moves on
tearing bark from the trees
browsing for lichen in sheltered places.
I sleep in a fur-bed, deep in time.
Dreaming of bisons and snakes
I move closer to the belly of my mother.

�**↗   ↗   ↗**

The world is very small, a mudball
wet in the shaping hand. The tribe explores
draws ridges and paths, ornaments the clay.
The women, daughters of poetry, gather
feathers and seeds
thread them on leather strips.
Meanwhile, the hunters invent sacred songs.
In their brains, a twist of consciousness
a new knowing. The web is started:
cat's cradle of intricate loops
that connect story to story, time to time.
I swing in it, dangle over the road
leading into the next age and the next
passing through Egypt and Persia
moving north. The voice calls before me.
No question, no answer: only the word
          "CHILD!"
cast out like bait. I snap at it
hold fast: an irresistible power
          reels me in.

"Behold, he is coming with the clouds!
Every eye shall see him!"   (Rev. 1:7)

NOTHING moves in the void
no eye burns in the socket of space
no voice speaks.
 —Patmos is an island-boat, an ark
 floating on cloudy waters.
 All time long, I heard the waves
 unrolling their ancient scrolls.
 I am sea-sick, night-sick and lonely;
 stars have drowned, fire sleeps
 in beeswax and flint.
 Yet, it is happening: in the East
 —will anyone believe—
 a body of light slowly rises.
Wake, brothers, sisters
uncover your faces, take
to the fox dance, the dolphin leap
the flight of the geese; stand, dancing
in the coming sun! Yes, I have seen:
here, where the mud will freeze into rock
through a million years of change
the Word is stamped down, stamped clear.
And this is the first message
 —morning news sent
 before mud-rims become
 lips of rocks:
 God is light
 a diamond point cutting
 through darkness, writing without pause
 inventing marvelous creatures, man and beast.
Are you listening?
 No, you are distracted
 by the noisy branching of time
 by the years soft-falling on the ground

exposing rotten flesh, blackened seed.
Like a dog with a bone
you hold death in your jaws
shaking it with growls of anger.
How long will you bark the same questions:
"Can we travel farther? Is there a path
out and around the skull-plate
beyond the last image
lastly printed on the brain?"
    STOP!
       Stop that pig-snouting in the dark!
Understand the way of the child
how it bursts through the birth-ring
takes the world in, easy as air.
Understand the lifting of the latch
       the turning of the lock
       the pushing open, the breaking through!
O Brothers, O Sisters
       go dancing into the light
       go, new and naked, into God!

"I turned and saw seven golden lampstands and surrounded by them a figure like a Son of Man."
(Rev. 1:12)

REALITY is not
in the eye of the beholder.
The tree lives deep, feeds
on its own fact; it rises
trunk, branches, crown
defining itself, cell by cell
leaf by leaf. I touch, feel
green life under my finger.
If I turn, the tree neither retracts
its roots, nor rolls up its leaves.
It goes on sucking the rain
pumping sap into every twig.
Yet, something is shared:
that marvelous green machine
does not stand alone, apart from my being.
Look at the world: a network
of interlocking pieces—bird in the nest
chick in the egg, pit in the plum.
Inside the earth, the white light
of crystals, the gold flecks.
Inside the stone, patterns of other ages
scripts of ferns a million years old.
I am here, at the end of summer
standing under a ripening tree.
But it is not all: there is more
more truth than the eye can meet.
When I sleep, another day begins:
elsewhere, a heron wakes among Chinese reeds.
I accept the sun, the moon, believe
in their distant traveling.
But the truth of the matter
is not entirely seen: other spaces

beckon, places one enters now and then
darkly and in darkest night, to see
a brightness, a shining as of snow
in the midst of seven golden lamps.

"These are the words of the First and the Last, who was dead and came to life again." (Rev. 2:10)

I speak.
  Power was given
  to form sounds, to name.
I have invented so many words
  bags and pouches
in which I stuff a world
  of images and scents.

"Cat," I say.
  Called, it runs
  to the milk poured in the dish.

"Tree," I say.
  It nods in the wind
  a wild, untamed thing;
  it lives outside its name
  ignoring the words I fit
  to bark, root and twig.
The sky fills with noises:
  flapping wings
  shrieking voices.
I must break through
  push, through the blue shell
  a fistful of prayers.

"Lord," I say.
  Time cracks open
  history lies flat, a map
  seen all at once:
  rivers and roads running
  in the same direction;
  people marching on and on
  passing through arc upon arc
  of life, death, rebirth.

"Lord," I say.
   I am plucked out
   lifted into soundless space.
   The tongue tries further speech;
   the mind furiously looks
   for clipped bits of phrases
   but words are shot down
   pierced by pellets of light.
What was it that I sought?
A pure language, a way
of speaking the truth
nothing but the truth.

Now silence is held to my lips
a hot coal, a perfect answer.

*"Your strength, I know, is small, yet you have observed
my commands and have not disowned my name."*
(Rev. 3:8)

I am old
a man having eaten his years
grain by slow grain, holding
the last one, hard between the teeth:
a kernel of no taste.
Prophecies? What words can spell
an old man's visions?
What food will calm the pangs
of his eternal hunger? Not fish soup!
Not a watery slop of common things!
I want the meat
of great mythical beasts:
let them come from the north
where they live hidden
under the snows of tribal memory;
let them shake their bearded masks;
let them grunt and buck their horns!
I will hear what they say
I will listen.

The sky is clear, empty;
the sea wears, green and silky
a ruffled gown.
What do I know?
Every pebble is a world of enigmas
every salt-crystal a city
with barred gates. I seek elsewhere
I stand by another door
begging entry, knocking.
I use eyes sharp as instruments
words shaped like hammers.
I beat upon the door of air
until my knuckles bleed

until my words crack
into bloody splinters.
Shall I die in ignorance, never to see
further than the outline
drawn in chalk:
shape of a dead man's fall?

God, look at my arms
at their bony branching;
look at my heart
that dry, leathery pouch!
Feed me, fill me again
with buzzing summer sounds.
I am your child
your fading image printed
on worn and tearing cloth.
Open to me!

"I saw an open door in heaven; and the voice that sounded like a trumpet said, 'Come up here, and I will show you what must happen after this.' At once, the Spirit took control over me. There in heaven was a throne with someone sitting on it. His face gleamed like such precious stones as jasper and cornelian; all around the throne there was a rainbow the color of emerald." (Rev. 4:1-3)

"Do not weep, for the Lion from the tribe of Judah, the Scion of David, has won the right to open the scroll and break its seven seals."   (Rev. 5:5)

YOU have seen the world
how it hangs in the butcher shop
bleeding on meathooks.
You have seen the trembling lamb
tied in the courtyard.
    —it was your neck in the noose
    it was your turn!

The rains came first
—forty days and forty nights—
unrolling from the sky
their dark webbing.
The rivers became sinewy beasts
enormous serpents coiled
around the land. They swallowed
farms and fields, thrashed about
on high ground. Words
could no longer be spoken:
they trickled like spit
from the lips of the dying.
There were no more voices
to tell who were these people:
men, women, children drifting by
forever sunk in water-sleep.
Centuries passed, and soon enough
it was Egypt, exile, toil;
mud packed in baskets
shouldered by slaves;
the harps mute in the willow trees.
How long before the signs lead us
to another age, another place?

Through countless turns of the earth
turns of speech, twists of road
the mind expanded to contain
the data of new skills
the names of things
experienced and remembered.

You are bound to ask, "How come?
Why are we back in the cave
haunted by the same ghosts:
ogres and elves casting on the walls
their grotesque shadows;
giant goat-herders barring the door
    and we the goats on a short rope
        waiting?"

You have seen the world slashed
drained of blood.
You have not seen enough
you have not looked:
there is a child born
in the strawbed of time;
there is a word born of God
in the human speech. It spells
freedom, abundance, peace.
Between our sobs and cries
you can hear the surging song
—the gravediggers, the pallbearers
stop in their tracks; death's grin
slips away from the mask.
It is over, it is all over:
the reign of the carrion
the vulture's feast, the rack
on which the world hangs bleeding!

The child speaks of innocence saved
of life grafted on lifeless limbs.

"What proof?" you ask. None
there is none to offer, none to need.
The future calls
and it is a child that beckons
that opens the way.

"There was silence in heaven." (Rev. 8:1)

WORDS began to fly early
their wings black
each feather an iron shaft
shot through the morning sun.
They entered the city, roosted
on chimney and bedpost
perched in cathedral and shop
sounding themselves into lectures
seminars, arguments and spats.
People walked the streets
dressed in skin and cloak
printed with all manners of names.
Words mated, multiplied, infested
every house, every room.
Some were killed by hunters
guardians of the city halls;
others collapsed, were caught
eaten innocently to fatten
further speech. They cried out
they shouted, they fell into whispers
to soar again, to bring forth
new generations of noises.
They entered drainpipes and arteries
clogged sewers and tear-ducts.
They were so enormously many
the city swelled, burst forth
in a great black scream.

I send you one Word
and it spells silence, nakedness.
It says, "Peel the stifling layers
push away the choking weights.
Go to quiet, hidden places

where you can hear the earth moved
by worm and mole, lifted
by the green muscles of new plants.
Gather the silence around you:
a downy cloth hanging loose
hardly touching the bruised flesh.
Enter silence, stretch yourself
through it, leap free!"

"The first angel blew his trumpet. Hail and fire, mixed with blood, came pouring down on earth." (Rev. 8:7)

SOMEONE pumps brass notes
like bullets in the air.
Hey, you sniper on the high roof
can't you see what you are doing?
Can't you be careful of the children
jumping rope in the streets? They leap
from age to age, counting rhymes
their bodies wedged into the future
pressed against the tide. They are
half between earth and sky.
Let them be! And the sleeping lovers
in the billows of sheets: they sail
through the gulfs and around the capes
their bed a raft of precious wood.
Let them be! Let the curtain fall smooth
around the window frame, let hands move
to touch, lips to kiss and speak.
Nothing much is going on:
just the ordinary business
of living here and now.
Give it time! The race toils
pushing itself up, one step
then another, over millions of years.
So take your trumpet
Angel, and come another day!

"Then I looked, and I heard an eagle that was flying high in the air say in a loud voice, 'Oh, horror, horror!' How horrible it will be for all who live on earth when the sound comes from the trumpets!" (Rev. 8:13)

ONE look at the world
and I am gripped
by a dark, devouring thing:
beak and claw tear me open;
I scream in the shuffle of iron wings.
A huge totem-beast eats my lungs
dips for the heart through bloody pools.
In its eye, the glimmer of weapons
the glint of breastplates and spurs.
Its breath is fire, a burning torch
high-blown by the wind. It speaks;
I see pale horses, pale riders
moving through its words:
"Horror, horror, horror," it says
sputtering sulphur and smoke.

Little children, beware of idols!

Stars drop, clanging like tin plates;
the moon stained with women's blood
rolls along the slant of time.
Warring tribes stream
through mountain passes, pour
over the continents—helmets
and spear-heads the only light.
The beast pulls the thread
dangling in the void: history unravels.
It is dangerous to be human:
the rifled tree lives on
the rabbit hides underground

rocks continue the eternity of stones
—but the children of man die
mangled by the monstrous beast.

Little children, beware of idols!

*"Now is the time to reward your servants the prophets,
your dedicated people, and all who honor your name,
both great and small."* (Rev. 11:18)

BLANK is the page
upon which I begin to write
the date, the day, the facts.
Word after word, I hold on
to the pen as time pulls
is pulling me away
further from this place
from this task.

But I have eyes
   eyes by the thousand:
   How they weep, how they glitter
   in their caves of flesh!
   How they flash, these jewels
   these liquid wounds!
   How they open
   toward the future
   toward the past!

Seeing, I speak
   dare say these real things
   over which time has no power.

When the world appears soundless
—by its choice, a clap of dream
in a bell of air—listen
   for the voices
   small hushed voices:
   the singers hidden, unseen.
Listen to the heartbeats:
   Life tapping a tune
   coursing through the ages

from woman to man
from man to woman.
Even when the lights go out
—lamps, candles and stars—
even in darkness, they speak
they speak together:
wonder, revelation, delight.
Listen! Even the pebbles sing
repeat in small stone voices
the holy name of God.

> *"Happy are those who are invited to the wedding-supper*
> *of the Lamb!"*   (Rev. 19:9)

ANIMAL blood stains my hand
the guts of a great celestial bird
soft-spill on the sand. I must eat.
The crabs hide, the sea foams
with a milk too bitter to suck.
I take to the hunt, spear
feathered images, roast them
on the spit of my need.
I eat through the world's flesh
tear it without apologies.
I am Everyman Adam sent from the garden
sent starving to this foreign beach.
So, I feed when I must, take it all in:
earth, sky, what flies and runs.
Filled, half-settled in sleep
I am still hollowed out
I am still enormously empty.
Somewhere, there is food
more potent than meat.
I do not turn to the past
follow the snake-root of being
for you are here, Lord:
I have seen you lift the dead
out of their shrouds, return sap
to the withered tree.
Bless my hunger, Lord:
        feed me!

*"And now I saw heaven open and a white horse appear;
its rider was called Faithful and True. . . . He is known
by the name Word of God. . . . On his cloak and on his
thigh there was a name written, the King of kings and
Lord of lords."*   (Rev. 19:11, 14, 16)

BOOKS are opened
    morning books printed
    with the names of ancestors
    with the world spelled out
    as a throne room
    built for a race of kings.

Books are opened
    evening books where the moon
    is a great mineral word
    a polished stone hung
    on the breast of space.
    —Night books where children sleep
    cradled in dreams; they slip
    through the rings of images
    through the pattern's chains
    to free their eyes, their hands
    to see, to touch
    beyond the written pages
    their real face, their true form.

Who speaks?
    In the distance
    chanting voices
    intone the story of a Man
    master of impossible crafts:
    his feet steady on the water
    his hands bleeding fire
    over the ground, his life
    a key forever pressed
    into death's lock.

Books are opened by the thousand
  each one a century, a moment
  through which he rides
  at an even clip. Hear
  the horse's hoofs clattering
  on the iron road of time!
  He speaks distinct words
  each one a flaming arrow
  flying straight, hitting home.
  He is here and there
  at once everywhere
  deep into the past
  high into the future, a Man
  with the eyes of his mother's tribe
  seeing once, seeing all
  in a single glance.
  He rides to the center of the target
  straight to the heart.
  His name is King of kings
    Lord of lords.

*"He was called the Word of God and the armies of heaven
followed on white horses, clothed in fine linen, clean and
shining."*   (Rev. 19:14)

THERE is a Word
   one letter, one sound
   loud spoken in time.
There is a Word
   one green bright note
   rolling into space
   pressing atoms together
   to form seed and spore and sperm
   to burst into kingdoms of plants
   and kingdoms of flesh.
There is a Word
   one sound held and sustained
   through ages of ice and iron
   —perfectly tuned, conceived
   eternally as a perfect pitch
   of what it is to BE.
There is one Word
   radiating snow-flakes and roses
   activating generations of whales
   slipping bird into bush
   fish into sea, man into woman.
Listen! The cosmos is chamber and shell
   in which the Word leaps
   dancing a dance of creation:
   every movement a moment in time
   a profusion of years
   piled up, decomposing, giving birth
   to a new processional of days.
Listen! The music of that one note builds
   body-sequences, marvelous machines
   full-pulsing, shaping whole sentences
   saying life, life, as the blood beats.

There is one Word:
   net-full of stars, cloth patterned
   with sea-and-land-scapes
   cloak of flesh
   around shoulder of bones.
Praise God!

"There shall be an end to death, and to mourning and crying and pain."   (Rev. 21:4)

BY dark-sliding waters, I watched;
they came to mind, descending
from the hilltops:
tourists of the planet
ready to rearrange the objects of the day.
To be is not a question:
they are, in vertigo and pain
holding on to things—fingers curled
around handles, gripping shovel, frying pan, axe.
No patience here, no sure virtue:
fury spills the pot, anguish
bites the heart, fear
madly barks at the shadows.
But this is it: our world.
Glued together scale by shining scale
the sun, that great luminous fish
swims in the morning sky.
Children are born while the compass needle
trembles, marking space; while the clock
works its pattern, stamps its numbers
upon the wall.
Can a man believe, can a woman know?
The frenzied, the blind, the limping
snake through the streets
coughing blood, hiding their sores
under layers of rags. I live in Patmos
dine on the syntax of the dazzling isle
while elsewhere children feast
on potato peels and rats.
Can I believe? The question
is a hook piercing my tongue.
I bleed, but say YES!

"Behold, I am making all things new!" (Rev. 21:5)

SOMETHING plays
    between the lines
something bright
    never stops flowing
    in and out of dark landscapes:
        threads of light spun
        from a golden fleece
        twisted together, played
        against a darker theme.

Blood crusts the sheets
    stains open, mortal thighs.
The newborn child sucks in
the world's bitter taste
    screams
as time rolls downhill
    faster and faster
a rough stone scraping
                scarring the skin.

Something plays, dances
    between the lines
    a robust spirit
    a fertile power pressing
    swollen seeds from dying bloom
    newborn babe
    from ancient human ways.
Blessed are those who believe!
They see life's thread pulled
    bright and silky
through the needle of death.
Their bones mend;
now and then, they see

—more than connections, correlations—
the whole dazzling pattern
the full script.

They live, live forever!

*"The city had no need of sun or moon to shine upon it:
for the glory of God gave it light, and its lamp was the
Lamb."*   (Rev. 21:23)

I am weary, wish to be silent
to burn the fat of words
to let them sizzle in the fire.
Will they give light
when the night comes in
with tar and feathers
to glue the world still?

I eat, I spit, I am sick
of the taste of speech.
I wish for silence:
to be ushered in a space
where nothing is heard
but air displaced
by infinite resonances
echoes thinned out
to soundless vibrations
saying peace, peace without end!

I bear the sign
of the Man who steps free
out of the sealing stone.
Behind him, the wrap of time
the worn skin of the past.
His finger stirs the sand
lifts dazzling atoms:
worlds of white light are born.

I want his steady touch
I want to stay with a knowledge
longer than time.

But over and again
I pass through the door
visit the great house of language
find bones, amulets
find mostly the word "pain"
a spike pushed through the flesh
within the bleeding wrist.

Somewhere between earth and heaven
there is a rising
a solar shine, a being
gold and fleshed
for which no name was ever found.
I see, I cannot speak.

There is silence
    through which the Light thunders!

> *"Then he showed me the river of the water of life, spark-*
> *ling like crystal, flowing from the throne of God and of*
> *the Lamb down the middle of the city's street."*
>
> (Rev. 22:1)

BITTER, bitter this place
scrap of land, raft
anchored among the waves.
Bitter, watered by tears
the words I write to take
the measure of the wind
the speed of images passing
with clouds, with time.

I am alone
    I am not alone:
in these immense fields
millions upon millions float
in primeval ooze, ready to be born.
Death, as a midwife, stands by
a nurse, gentle of hands.
And what am I among these people:
a speck lifted by brooms of air
a flake melting in the heat?
The dust rises, the sun falls
on the shoulders, heavy
like a yoke of brass.

I prayed the Lord, held his name
hot and glowing in my soul
and I saw
    not with the eyes of a stranger
    but of a son coming home in the evening
    by paths of guiding stars.
I heard my name called
out of time, in a tongue
I perfectly understand.

Dark, it is said, dark is God's dwelling
but I saw it clear
saw it with naked eye
a space without volume
without length or height
—nothing about it in any book—
and I lay still and glad
a little sparrow
in the feather-nest of God.

What name, what word, what sound
can match that pure feeling?
I could say there was a city
carved from a single crystal
—the light within neither fire nor lamp—
but it would be a second print
of a first truth, a shadow
of what is shadowless.

I am alone, rooted on this shore
and the waters crackle
and the sun spreads its red ink
floats like a jelly-fish
on the surface of the sea.
There is no door at which to knock
no stone to turn, no house to enter.
My eyes are opened, my old eyes
brimful of old images, painted
by many years of knowing the truth
in a certain human way.
I keep watch, I pray:
"Lord of this small planet
and of, smaller, this estate
of ivory and skin
    remember me in your kingdom!"

"The Spirit and the Bride say, 'Come!'" (Rev. 22:17)

SCRIPT on the paper
words rounded like ant eggs
white and fat
    saying what?

It is the end of time:
darkness clicks shut
a giant lid tightly fitted
over the rim of space.
Once, there was a city
glittering with the fire of women
with the light of their breasts.
Once, there were children in the womb
alive, delicately curled
like ferns in early spring.
Once, there were people
knowing the right use
of iron and salt—makers of tools
builders of temples.

Now, there are fragments of flesh
sticking to bark and stone.
All the postcards have been sent:
Goodbye! Bon voyage! Adieu!
Brother, sister, father, mother
they are droplets in the air
shadow-prints upon exploded walls.
The tiger, the elk, the bear:
their ancient images are locked
in charred books. The reign
of the cockroach begins.

There will be a new earth
    and a new heaven:

the Spirit and the Bride say
"Come!"

They will be ready
they will come
    out of broken picture-frames
    out of albums, letters, yellowed telegrams
    —Get well! Rise and shine! Soon
      very soon—
    out of burial mounds
    out of the drowning sea
    and the sucking swamps:
      mothers with children in their arms
      lovers entwined
      all going to light, speaking
      good words related to real things.
It is not, hazy and slow-winding
a dream from which to wake
sorry and sad:
it is the truth, the whole truth
summed up in one Word eternally spoken
    —and all life lives on
      in its sound.

*"Come forward, you who are thirsty; accept the water of
life, a free gift to all who desire it."*   (Rev. 22:17)

WATCH
    when there is no sound
    for the sound of cloth tearing
    smooth and long: a shroud
    being rent from within.
Something free is being born!

If you look
    through the dull shine of time
    through the glass misted over
    by centuries of rain
you will know: this Man is gone
who was carried deep into the rock.
He is walking in the blue morning
    cracking death, that word of stone
    between the wheels of his hands.
He walks masterless in a world
where people move by bullwhip
    —the fine tip barely touching the skin
    but the threat real and pressing.

He sees the trembling faces
    fragile crystal faces:
    they break so soon, fall
    into a thousand frozen pieces
    —here an eye forever fixed
    there a mouth forever trapped
    voiceless under the ice.

Take the bread, he says
eat yourself full of life
    —strong the light over the world—

Take this whole marvelous sun of bread
   this whole full circle ever circling
   container of planets and stars
   earth and heaven. Eat!
And drink deep, beloved
   drink to sleep and to waking
   in the blue morning
   where I walk
     masterless, free.
Come with me!

CATHERINE de VINCK

A BOOK OF HOURS

TO BROTHER THOMAS

CONTENTS

A BOOK OF HOURS

MATINS

BLACK
  bitter night.
The only tools, modest clubs
    needles of bone pulling leather strips
    through the gap of millenia.
Light, uninvented, sleeps
    in cloud and flintstone.

"A":

Alpha of unconsciousness
Adam standing up
    —his fur shed
    brilliantly naked—
    crosses the boundaries
    filters through time's slits and cracks
    in a paradise of awakening.

What signs?
    The carved rock, the bloody gut
    prophecies of the masked dancer:
he runs here in the street
    climbs stairs
    crashes through the door
    falls through layers of sleep.
What moves behind his eyelids?
Landscape of flood, disaster, fire
juxtaposition of water and flame
animals swimming
    pale and magical
        in his head.

41

In the beginning
　　darkly
the child sucks its thumb, holds
　　the secret of the world
　　the amazing numbering of the stars:
sight, touch, the power to name
　　to rage, weep, love.
Eternal, enchanting, life moves
　　head-first
through the great chambers of the world
towards the likeness of man.
Shall the womb be scraped
　　language killed
　　the voice clipped
　　　　before the first sound can rise
　　　　and become song?

Night hangs at the window
　　a square of black silk
　　drawn over the face, hiding all
　　but the living eyes.
On the outer side:
　　movement in the grass
　　hunger of lions
　　thirst of rasping tongues
　　　　coming to the garden pool.
On the inner side
　　within the soul's passages
　　ancient roots work their way
　　through mortar and stone
—a greening stem
a great hook of knowledge
　　pierces the mind.
Revived, delivered
　　into the words of our waking
what do we say
　　but contradicted good-mornings

what do we show
    but contractions of fingers
    over knobs of sleep?

Lord
    open the shutters of time
      the gateway of speech.
When we leave the night's cave
shall we remember the dream-house
    dream-city through which we passed
    counting birthdays, counting death
    by fire, flood, tormented wishing?
What was handed to us
    through dark vaporous doors?
What password, skill, sign
    from what outreaching past?

Lord
    see these cold words change
    from deep to pale color
    as the future begins to shine
    in brilliant prophecies:
a power, bright and blowing
    shakes the crown of flowering trees;
stars leave us, the moon turns away
    to lift other seas.

Lord
    we come
      into the dailiness
      of bread, room, street.

Bless us
    as the bird of dawn sends
    to our waking brain
    a first needle of sound.

PRIME

FROM the turned page
   in the book of creation
words fatten into substantial forms:
let there be light!
And light comes to the hand
   the aluminum roof, the milk
   in the glass pitcher on the table.
In the tree
   green with life before time
   the bird of the first stanza
   begins to sing:
   music shapes the world
   feathers house the new day.
Structured bodies in structured rooms:
   bone answers beam
   eye measures the distance.
Shall we walk on the penciled line
   holding what we own
   in precise equilibrium
or shall each moment be invention
   a fleshing act:
      words over the spine of thoughts
      skin over rushing blood
      color coating common facts
      violet for sorrow
      red for love?
On the huge canvas
   the aurora becomes an imperative
   a power forcing out of earth and wood
   a world of resonance, an art
   hatched whole and living.
Water washes over us
   a loose, flickering thing

rising from sacred deep caves
to enfold, to cling, to fit us
skin-tight in silver chill.

We live by association
    by the curve and turn of images:
Where has it dripped away
    the time when good-morning held
    the roundness of a child waking
    to oatmeal and sea-sounds
        —water-bells of the waves
      gong in the heart of the shell?
The lost garden is a pin point on the map:
    where are the flamingos and the peacocks
    hand-fed tigers and monkeys?
Eve, that odd, unremembering woman
    comes to the breakfast table
        offering
           with coffee
              an apple half-eaten.

Lord
    the summer crackles underfoot.
    The winter to follow
    will be stone, hard against the knuckles.

Lord
    does the subway mouth lead
    to your underground
    to the gold vein of your love
    the sapphire of your speech?
    Or shall it bring us dead-center
    in the wrong of hellish pain
    —throat slit, pockets picked clean of hope?

Lord
    bless this day
        for you, beyond counting;

for us, a small uncertain measure
a spoon dipped in a protean sea.
Yet, how can this be
that we are mad with the thrill
of seeing the sun lit:
fire restored
lamp set high, set firmly in the mind
revealing durations, epochs
all ages and norms of man?
Seeing is believing:
Lord, we know!

LAUDS

FORTY days and forty nights
   through the desert:
we walk from past to future
   shedding the fleece of old
   leaving the meat stewing
      in the clay pots of Egypt;
   moving where
      —quails in the wind
      corn-flakes in the morning—
   where the opening sea
      the cloud
         the fire-pillar
            show the way.
Daylight falls still in the room
   where bed, chair, glass
   the rose bleeding on the table
   settle in solid utterances.
We enter the fold of garments
   the hollowness of sleeves
adjust over eye and mouth
   the pigments of the ceremonial mask.
Groomed and shod, we are ready
   to pass through an imagined door
   to enter a new world.

Something moves through the cloud
   a voice moves alive
   moves life into flesh
            into man, woman
            into the sparrow's throat
            and the seed's core.
Shall we drive on
   past these rocks shaped

by fingers of sand
or choose a single stone, altar
    to offer aromatic wood, a handful of fire?
We come
    with disconnected words:
        "Light"
            we say;
                "Lord"
                    we say
    offering the crackling manna
    pouring the milk of dreams
    into the breakfast bowl.
The desert has sifted its crystals
    into our blood: we carry these particles
        —silence, solitude, wild wishing—
    in the ache of our soul.

Lord
    in the country of the morning
we row the sandy rivers
    choking on dust and smoke.
The walls
    —of animal skins
    stretched on crossed poles—
    can be folded, carried
    a thousand miles against the wind.
Memories glimmer
    jingle like coins
    in our pocket.
We breathe time
    in and out
stretch our arms
    like branches to the sun.

Lord
    yes, we praise thee!

TERCE

DARK-hearted with seeds
   sunflowers line the garden path.
Yes, we have seen the pleasant house:
   pears on the windowsill
   coffee on the table
   books, green plants, a new fire
      growing under bundled twigs.

Lord
   can we break the crust of this day
   can we lift the cup, drink this hour
     before it turns brackish and brown
     seeps away through the cracking glaze?
Over and over, we twined
   one moment to the next
our hands steady
   trying for a pattern never held before.
Twisted in the love-knot of your making
hidden in the form of your secret
   we are
     Lord
      naked only in your sight.
Through all these rooms
   —small and smoked
     mere chinks in the face of the rock—
we move bone to bone
   breast to breast
   dressed in each other's speech
   in the silk of our mutual giving.

Lord
   we have thieved:
   in the ancient distance
     apple of succulence

first knowing of misuse
             of disconnection
sweet morning fruit
golden intelligence flashing
the fortune of its thoughts:
(*"Our* knowledge," we say
adding another coin
to the careless heap.)

Behind us:
glitter, mortality, pain!
Before us:
glitter, mortality, pain!
Yet, so many years in the finding
this one clear space
this place where planets and pebbles
             animals, flowers, men
mesh in the convergence of your sight!

We speak
we are spoken.
We call
we are called
and the voice never fails
but increases
changes from one intensity to another
forming new sounds:
             "O"
of wonder, of openness
gold disk, ornament of winter
gate to let in
             O your Sun!

SEXT

EARTH eroded, stones shifting
tigers nearly extinct
  and time?
Time waterfalls away from us.
In the melting noon
  all things drop
  ripe and open
  fruits of the half-way
  to be eaten on the road
  before the whistle blows.
Where are we?
  Is the day a coil around us
      a locking circle?
  Or is it set deep in an ancient wall
  a window looking out
    towards pastures
        beribboned children
           legions of angels?

O world of common sight
  of sweat and cry, argument and tension
  penumbra that calls light:
here we are
  home in the green shade of the maple
  patterning the dust with our weight
  pecking with the sparrows
    the crumbs of the past.
We came from buried cities
  from the pits where bones are gathered
  wing-bones, antlers, tail-rings and tusks;
we came from the formlessness of water
  from the curve and twist of millennia
    the bending of the bow, the arrow flying. . . .

We came together, many-voiced
  and the stories we tell
    recounted from age to age
  hang in the air like scrolls
    unrolling in waves of color:
  smoke-blue for all the cooled worlds
    of men and beasts and plants;
  black for the tears we shed
    through a thousand and one nights;
  green for the grass-nests
    where lovers in each others arms
      summon the future.

Lord
  the stones of morning
  —clean-washed stoops over which
  so eagerly we tread—
  gradually darken; our shadows
  fall limp at our feet;
  we pull them
    —shadow-bodies
  shadow-worlds.
With every step
  we haul their leaded weight.

Lord
  hidden in ourselves
  hunger screams
  thirst rakes the chalky riverbeds
    of rainless countries.
Let us find the swollen hive
  the honey-well of meaning.
We seek beyond scrawls and garbled words
  beyond the sign engraved
    on the face of the rock
the secret of the light we cut and cross:
secret of man ascending the ladder of being

through what ruptured link
holding what guiding thread?

Huddled against the earth's brown skin
we hear a muffled rhythm:
    beyond the proof of experience
    a remembered unknown song
      life-charged, wind-full
    lifting the smell of pitch
    from the pits
    speaking the names of dead hunters
    calling the gatherers of berries
        the pluckers of wild apples.
They come, keep coming
    in the long pause of noon
drumming words of a communal song
rubbing sticks till the flame leaps
    blue and crested
out of their distant hands
to warm the present day.

Lord
    keep us still
    as time turns on its hinges
    like a creaky door.
We cannot go on forever
    lifting the ram's horn
    to blow our screeching questions.
Hold us in soundlessness
    with mind polished
      a brass mirror in which faintly at first
      a reflection appears
      an imprint intensified
        from moment to moment
        from year to year
      till suddenly we catch
        without touch or sight

the full slant of your hidden sun.
What we see on waking
  —shape, place, the stand
  of habitual trees—
  retains its literal form:

September stains the woods: ferns are yellowing, and on the slope where stones have marvelous dark eggplant skins, water runs cooler, slips a silver chill through the grass. In the blurring haze, the house looks brown-feathered, an old hen brooding in a weedy yard. We are fingers, hands, legs at work in fast-moving traffic—clouds in the sky, cars on the road, rotating planets. We are silk knots of nerves set within delicate organic shells; we are ash and limestone. Hello, goodbye! We grope through rarefied air along tracks of vibrant energy. All of it, the allness of all kingdoms, the juice of the universe, nectar of unknown stars, of barely perceptible cells, flow into a cup hollowed out of clay, sky and stone. We press it to our lips, O Lord of the Meridian, and drink.

NONE

TIREDNESS sets in the bone
    deep like an axe.
We have not seen the land
    promised to our tribe;
we roamed the wilderness
    leaving neither script nor track
    carrying our life, its weight
    of leather and rag
    through time's rippling waves.

Home
    is a million miles away
and what we hear, the news
    of distant battles, the cries
    of burning children
roars in our brain:
    small ghosts of supplication
    they beg through enormous spaces
    for soothing oil, a bandage
    a cup of oblivion.
It is not flesh that fills
    suit or dress or glove
but an infinite number of grains:
    sand-man   sand-woman
      we stand
blind and still
while the wind moves the world
transporting huge chunks of land
    whole cities, centuries and ages
from one dark place to another.

Smell, sight, touch:
    we long

for the brew in Egypt's pots,
   herbs, onions, lamb
the pause by the campfire
the idle talk of noon.
Who will come to us in this hour
   with lips of water
   liquid fingers
   river hair?

Lord
   we thirst!
There are no watering places
   on the moon, no pail or spoon
   to dip in the milk
   of that beautiful face.
We need no abstract terms
   cold knife of logic
   iron pincers of thoughts
   forged in hellfire.
We need no smear of moondust
   on insulated boots:
we need the earth's moisture
   the mothering ooze
   fertile womb on which to rest
   at ease and in pleasure.
We need the touch of others
   the clasping arms
   the joined hands.
We need beauty
   —she of the carved granite
   palace-figure with jeweled lid;
   she of music, poetry
   constellated with images
   resonant like bell-metal!
We need
   eyes to see

the other side of life:
what we wear close to the skin
   that rough and prickly cloth
   that wool spun with brambles
is not the whole garment.
At times, we finger the silk
   of a celestial cloak;
we hold handfuls of a fabric
   woven on a loom stretched
   from north to south, manned
   by the four servants of the wind.

GOD
   we need you!
Heal what we keep hidden
   under the thousand folds
   of our perpetual smiling:
the slashed heart
the mind grown slack
   soft under its shell
   and like the crab, burrowing
   to dark retreats.

Lord
   with a hand that is no hand
      but a diamond of shattering light
follow the contour of our pain
cut, deepen the wound
   till it becomes a door to your mercy.
Much is discomfort here:
   gritty sand mixed with manna
   the space for language
   crowded with careless words
   and hope narrowed to the sight
   of an undulating belly
   in the next oasis of the mind!

Lord
we have moved horizontally
    all over an empty land.
Now we pause to gather the black thorn
    to build a fire on the stony slab
        of this hour.
We need a sign:
Shall it be other
    than the buzzard's circling
more than the bloody stain
    of the westering sun?
It is enough
    to be
        to say
            Lord!

VESPERS

LONG rope uncoiled
  sleeping serpent
  no flute can charm
the hour lies dark and still.
"A thousand years is like a day," says the Lord.
  Yesterday
slipping our hands
under the rock, we caught small crabs
for our supper; the place is lost:
we do nor recall the stream;
our other ancient face
curtained by millennia, recedes
  in the wrinkled water.
Time drops
  from what height
  into what endless depth?
Yesterday
  our daughters shaped the world
  to the roundness of their breasts;
today
  their breath freezes
    into snow-flowers
    white roses of cold metal.
Our sons' eyes were jewels
  embers glowing in the fiery masks.
Their dreams formed a maze
  a network in which to trap
    deer and buffalo.
Today
  they do not know the earth
    as nurse and woman.
They come home
  and life is a key in a determined slot

the turning of iron into wood
the coming into a room
where table, chair, food
are wild devouring powers.

Lord
    it was given to us to dance
        with the swelling of the buds
        the growing of the leaves;
    to invent rhythms, improvise sounds
    build a temple which would hold
        country, metropolis, planted field.
Now, we buy five stalks of wheat
    —dried, the heads drooping—
and nail them to a wall!
Who shall buy the wind?
Who shall touch the rising moon
    with rubber stamp or leather boot?
Who shall wear moon-chips
    as ornaments on neck-chains?

Lord
    what will happen
    already happens now:
    the idle fact, fattened
    by numberless numbers, multiplied
    added infinitely to the sum of itself:
    stone upon stone, bone upon bone
    dust over dust:
        death
            nothingness
                black death!

Lord
    keep the bear and the crow
    away from our flesh; deliver us
    from the lion's jaw.

In the night, they come hungering
to the bed where we lie
   folded upon ourselves
   knees up to chin
   rolling down huge mountains of sleep.
They wait among the image-trees
   dream-animals, spirit-hunters
    leaving real tracks
    inflicting real wounds.

Lord
   let us know
    even at this late hour!
The world is warm with your flesh:
water, fire, earth and air—your holy flesh
   vanquished and resurrected
   dying and ever-born
   cracking the stone open
   breaking the doors of death
    rising
   forever rising!

Lord
   this is our future:
    written in the palm's lines
    in the contour of every pebble
    in every rain-drop and cloud-shape.

We live
   not by imposed laws
   by grim deadly edicts
   but by that word which is freely spilled:
    love-seed in the sower's hand
   and the furrow wide open
    moistened by a long-ago stream.
Blessed are you
   Lord God of all creation!

Blessed are you
   for the ground of our dying!
Dust shall not sift into our sealed eyes
   shall not reach our flesh's ragged pockets.
By the door of our leaving
   you are
      setting us aswim in your saltless sea!

COMPLINES

WE read by the lamp:
   the wick slowly sucks the oil
     feeds the flame
   even as we now draw fire
     pluck the small lights of words
     from the turned page.

This time
   —open space to which we come
   surfacing with root-strength—
this time shall not be lost or found
   only transcended
     carried over and out
     of its perpetual turn.
On the other side of the wall
   —fox, beaver, otter, bear—
they call our animal spirits
   to the moon's radiant wells.
"Come," they say, "be reborn in a dream."
But continents throb around us
   centuries stand in circles
   and history is on our mind:
     the vast panorama of acts and laws
     the vision rearranged a thousand times
     by the born child, the dead man.

We have hands other than to touch
   eyes other than to see;
and the light we force
   out of oil and sticks
shines dark before the candelabra
set high on the templed stone of this hour:
seven-branched and all-knowing
   it drips hot with God's wax.

The sound, a monotone of voices
    word-pellets upon the skin of silence;
the sound pulls the snake out of its coils.
The emblems on its shield
display directions: it will lead us
if we wish, to the old quarry
    the cave velvet-hung with bats
where it will grow out of itself
and around us: an iron ring
    an absolute clasp
        from which there is no breaking.

Lord
    cut the knotted syntax of the beast
        —wars, tortures, killings
        are locked in its speech:
        daily, the world gets on
        with the deadly business!

Lord
    where are delight, revelation, wonder
        the spirit of the dance
    —man dancing in and out
        of the seriousness of events
    wearing laughter
        like an ultimate cosmology:
    the twinkle of stars on his face
    the sun's blinking eye shining
        clear through his pain?

Lord of lichen and bark
    of mushroom and goldenrod
crush the shell and seed of our days
mix the pigments and press them
    bleeding-wet into the shape of your praise.
Are we more than sparrows
    more than an eyelash curve and shade?

If we must sum up
   the talk and the deed
   —Lord, this is the midnight
   of our trembling—
let our naked truth fall like a stone
speed on forever in the abyss of your mercy.

It is late: the flame, for lack of oil
   now eats the wick
   feeds on our soul's tender marrow.
When shall we know
   without lense or lamp
the reality of the real?
     We are
these bodies silver and gold
overlaid by everlasting brightness.
The great pell-mell of the hive
the buzzing sound of the swarm
conceal the master-plan
   the honey mounting in the structured cell.
Time makes a curve, draws
a hazy circle around us
tells
   —but it lies—
the alphabet we spell
the script over which we labor
dissolves equally in water or fire.
Tells
   —but it is the ghost of a truth—
the house we build day by day
is of air and spidery webbing:
rain bears down on the roof
the beams rot and through the floor
the mandragora, the man-shaped root
   pushes its blind power.

When the prince of death appears
at the window, wagging a bony finger
   —Oh, the time will be ripe:
  we shall not die forever—
our hearts shall send out rays
outreaching the dark as we say

   LORD
     INTO YOUR HANDS
       WE COMMEND OUR SPIRIT.

19 78

SET IN ELEVEN POINT TIMES ROMAN AND EIGHT
POINT ITALIC AND PRINTED BY THEO. GAUS, LTD.
BROOKLYN, N. Y. TWO HUNDRED AND FIFTY
COPIES BOUND IN CLOTH AND SEVEN-
TEEN HUNDRED AND FIFTY COPIES
PERFECT BOUND CONSTITUTING
THE ORIGINAL EDITION